The Complete Scottish & English Country Dance Master for Recorders

PART ONE

The Spring Garden

by

Patricia M. O'Scannell

Cover credit: Barbara Mendelsohn

1 2 3 4 5 6 7 8 9 0

© 2002 BY MEL BAY PUBLICATIONS, INC., PACIFIC, MO 63069.
ALL RIGHTS RESERVED. INTERNATIONAL COPYRIGHT SECURED. B.M.I. MADE AND PRINTED IN U.S.A.
No part of this publication may be reproduced in whole or in part, or stored in a retrieval system, or transmitted in any form
or by any means, electronic, mechanical, photocopy, recording, or otherwise, without written permission of the publisher.

Visit us on the Web at www.melbay.com — E-mail us at email@melbay.com

The Complete Scottish and English Country Dance Master
for Recorders, Part I

Table of Contents

Dedication 3	The Hole in the Wall 30
Author's Preface 3	In the Fields of Frost and Snow 31
Foreword 4	Jack's Health 32
Notes on the Dances 4	Jack's Maggot 33
Acknowledgements 5	Joy After Sorrow 34
About This Book 5	Knole Park 36
Illustrations 5	Lord Howe's Jig 37
The Bishop 6	Long Live London 38
The Alderman's Hat 8	Love's Triumph 40
The Boatman 9	Lulle Me Beyond Thee 42
The Bunch of Rushes 10	Mr. Beveridge's Maggot 43
Childgrove 11	Mr. Cosgill's Delight 44
Christchurch Bells 12	Mr. Isaac's Maggot 45
The Clansman 13	Mrs. Savage's Whim 46
The Comical Fellow 14	Orleans Baffled 47
Confesse 16	Parson's Farewell 48
Dick's Maggot 17	St. Andrew's Fair 49
Epping Forest 18	St. Margaret's Hill 50
Easter Thursday 20	Sellinger's Round I 51
Fain I Would 21	Sellinger's Round II 52
The Fair Quaker of Deal 22	Spring Garden 53
The Female Saylor 23	Tribute to the Borders 54
Fentalarich 24	Sun Assembly 56
Gathering Peascods 26	The Spring 58
Hambleton's Round O 28	Trip to Paris I 60
The Hen and All Her Broth 29	Trip to Paris II 62

Dedication

Over the years I have had the pleasure of working with many fine musicians, dancers, dance-reconstructionists, and both early and country dance ensembles. One of the most delightful and creative people I ever met in this society of artists was Carl Whitman. Carl was the guest dance director at the Oregon Shakespeare Festival for my very first year there. He showed a love for this genre that is seldom seen, and burned with a curiosity and a creativity that was to be marveled at. His easy, laid back, and gentle style belied the fiercely detailed scholarship that was its background. He was one of the few individuals whom I have ever observed who combined both the intellectual and artistic, as well as "down to earth" social aspects of historic dance, to create something of great depth and grace. His own artistry as a dancer came into play with every decision he made, but also the most obvious and often overlooked questions were always foremost in his mind. Why did people dance? What was the purpose of these gatherings? What was the significance of a certain date? What did the patterns and figures represent? What could the titles tell us about the dances? Carl was a virtual treasure-trove of such information, and delighted in the details. We became fast friends, discussing (among other things) politics, art, philosophy (Carl was also extremely opinionated), and we had a weekly tea date when we spoke German together. He studied recorder with me and taught me English and Scottish country dancing, often inviting me to local gatherings. (Carl had lived "on the land" in the southern Oregon area for many years.) After he left the Ashland area, we remained friends for many more years, collaborating on workshops and talking about his book. Tragically, Carl died far too young in the late 1980's. He will never be replaced and is sorely missed. There will not be another one like him, for he showed us how to see a whole world inside of a tiny scrap from the past. I dedicate this book to his memory.

Pat O'Scannell
Spring, 2002
Ashland, Oregon

Author's Preface

These arrangements were written during a period spanning from 1980 - 1990. I hope they will be fun and instructive for both the beginner and advanced recorder player, as they were arranged for ensembles that contained many levels of ability. Although many parts were written for and played on recorders, the arrangements originally used a variety of instruments from harpsichord to hammer dulcimer, and from fiddle to clarinet. I hope this book will become a part of the aspiring country dance musician's library, as well as that of the many country dance ensembles that exist throughout the world. In this genre of music, tune and dance is expressed in the very specific tune that goes with it. This is unlike other dance forms where any number of tunes may be called upon to be used with a given dance. I hope that my arrangements stay always true to the essence of each dance, and help to underline it. Most of the dances exist only as single-line melodies, so you can use them as a starting point and have fun creating your own arrangements.

Foreword

Many dance masters and publishers have issued collections of dances and tunes for country dancing throughout the last four centuries. Country dances are popular to this day, and many groups in the United States and England still gather to enjoy them. I have given the sources for the dances in this book, many of which are also issued in modern collections, in the hopes that these lovely arrangements will inspire people to dance as well as to play and listen. The dances are accessible to all, from young dancers through old, with easy steps and harmonious, satisfying patterns. Their popularity is partly due to the beautiful melodies which accompany them, and partly to the sense of community that develops as the dancers meet and interact with one another in the patterns of the dances. These symmetrical and interwoven paths, first drawn in the late Renaissance and modified only slightly down through the centuries, allow everyone to participate equally, creating a feeling of communal enjoyment that has kept these dances live and vital up through the present day.

—Judith Kennedy

Notes on the Dances

The following abbreviations which appear above the individual arrangements refer to books and manuscripts from which many of the dances in this collection are taken.

Playford refers to a series of books first entitled *The English Dancing Master,* and subsequently *The Dancing Master,* published by John Playford of London and his successors, containing country dances and their tunes. The first edition appeared in 1651, and the last, the 18th, was probably published some time shortly after 1728.

Thompson refers to a series of short dance collections issued annually from 1774 to 1779 by Charles and Samuel Thompson, also of London. There were 24 dances in each collection.

Young refers to two collections (each in two or more editions) compiled by John Young, and published in London between 1713 and 1728. The first was titled *The Dancing Master: Vol. the Second,* and the other *The Dancing Master...the Third Volume.* Other sources are identified as clearly as possible throughout the text. I have attempted to give the earliest date that each dance appeared, but in some cases a dance may have appeared in a slightly earlier source. I am indebted to an unpublished manuscript by Carl Whitman for many of these attributed dates, as I am also indebted to him for the inspiration that he gave so many of us as a scholar, musician and sensitive, joyous dancer.

—Judith Kennedy

Acknowledgements

I would like to take the time to thank the people who were instrumental to the creation of this book. Carl Whitman, of course, who continues even after his death to be a great mentor and inspiration. I hope that his spirit beams down on me in approval of my efforts to bring this wonderful genre more into the consciousness of the popular culture. Judy Kennedy, who among many other things, is partly responsible for my opportunity to direct music at the Oregon Shakespeare Festival, and whose expert guidance has been indispensable to me throughout the years. In addition, she is a very sweet and generous person whose humbleness belies the vast store of knowledge about this genre of dance which she posseses. To Brooke Friendly and Chris Sackett who helped us much in documenting the origins of these dances; to Glenda Rackliff, who over the years brought me in to work with the Heather and Rose Country Dance Ensemble, where I directed music for balls and workshops, and wrote many of the arrangements found in this volume; and also to Bruce and Jocelyn Hamilton, for their aid in researching the dances. Special thanks are due to Steve Bacon and Todd Barton, who joined us in reading through the arrangements on recorders. Last, but not least, thanks to Sue Carney, my partner in all aspects and phases of putting this book together, and whose beautiful arrangements will be featured in future publications. Without her, I could not have accomplished the formidable task of completing such an ambitious project. —PO

About This Book...

Throughout this edition, the recorders best suited to the part are indicated to the left of the first measure. The abbreviations *sop* and *ten* refer to soprano and tenor recorders; '*nino* likewise stands for sopranino. The melodies are not always found in the top part. When in doubt, look for the asterisk to the left of the first measure to identify the melody line. Often, two different instrumentations, high and low, are suggested. In these cases, stick to one instrumentation or the other to avoid odd-sounding part transpositions. Sometimes, a section will be written in two octaves. In these places it may be advisable, depending upon your technique and the quality of your instrument, to play the lower part.

Illustrations

Most of the illustrations in this book are taken from *1800, Woodcuts by Thomas Bewick and His School*, edited by Blanche Cirker, Dover Publications, Inc.

Other Dover sources include: *Rustic Vignittes for Artists and Craftsmen, Animal Illustrations* and *Handbook of Renaissance Ornaments*.

Cover art by Barbara Mendelssohn.

Thompson Collection, 1778

The Bishop

arranged by
Patricia M. O'Scannell

𝅗𝅥 = 120

"Miss Dollard's Delight"

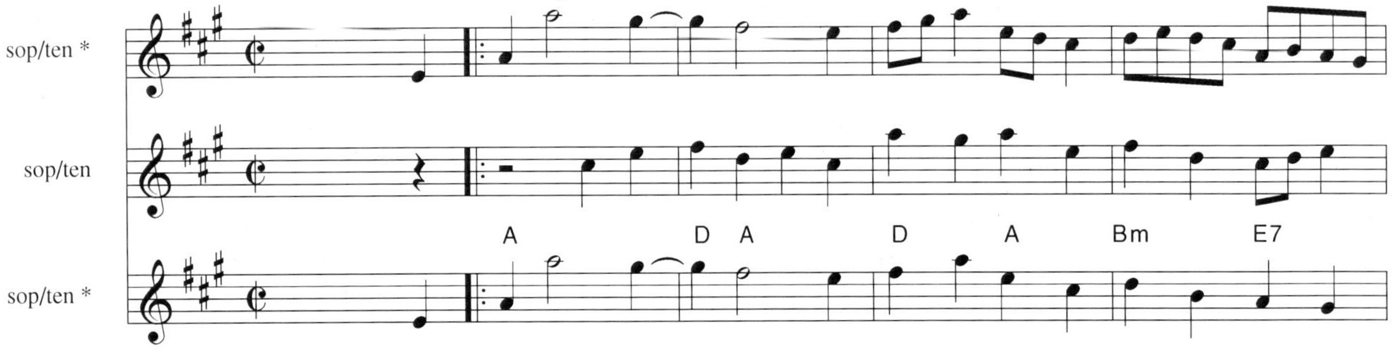

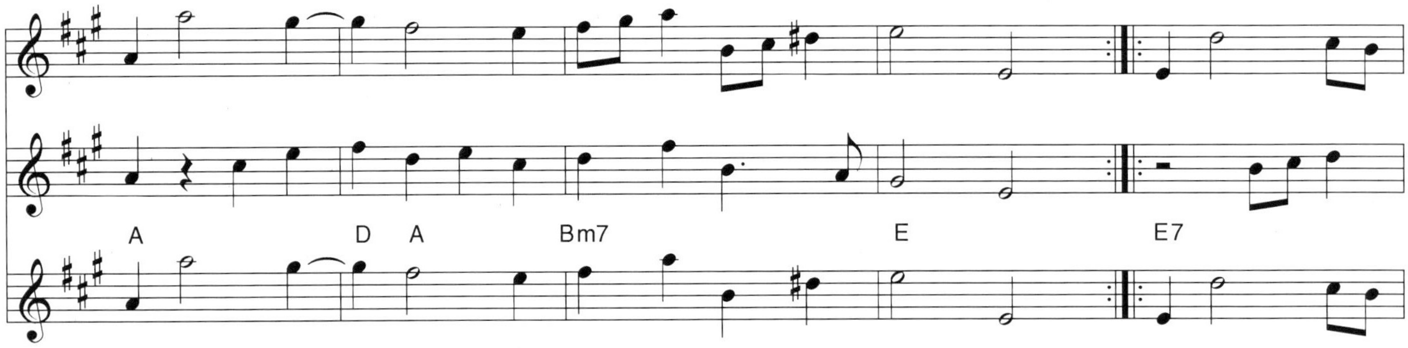

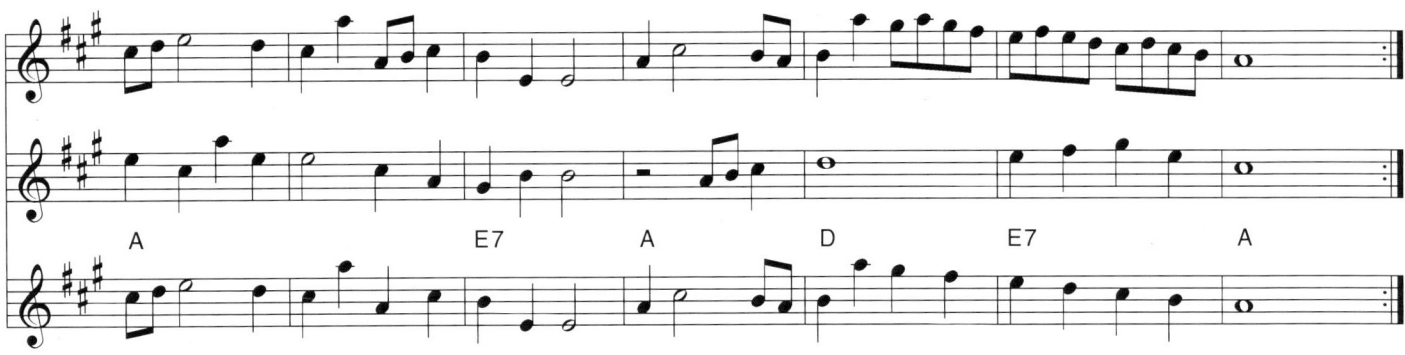

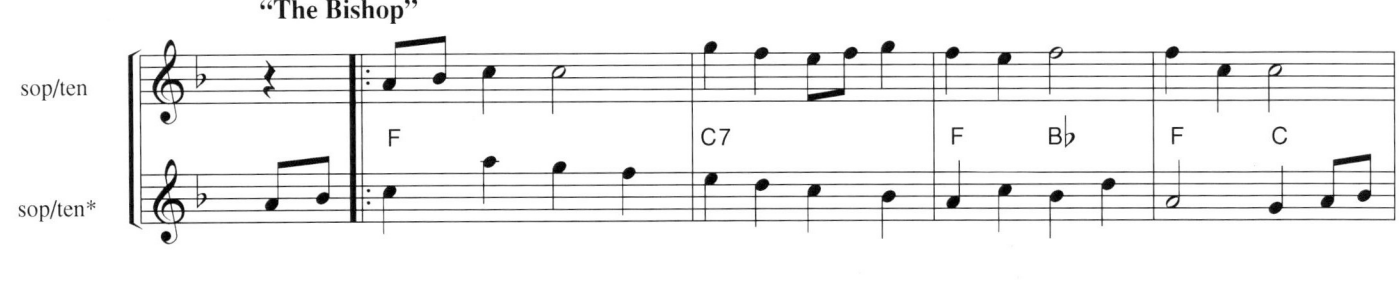

"The Bishop"

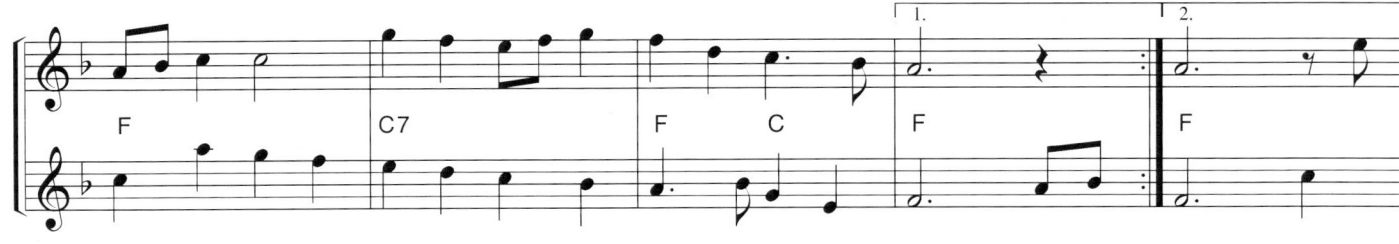

These two tunes, played consecutively, comprise the dance known as *The Bishop*. It is a favorite among English Country dancers, and is a lively and friendly dance. I can almost see Carl's beaming smile as he progresses toward me in the dance with the welcoming inclusiveness that marked his interpretation of this communal dance form.

Mrs. Dollard's Delight is both playful and compelling, and if taken at a proper clip and with crisp articulation (a "T" tonguing may be employed on strong beats), will be an exciting interpretation of this upbeat dance. The top line is an embellished version of the melody, so play it or the bottom part, but not both simultaneously. The second tune, *The Bishop,* is mellower and in the key of F, providing casual contrast to the first. Play it more smoothly to bring out the stepwise motion in the melody.

The Alderman's Hat

Thompson Collection, 1775

arranged by
Patricia M. O'Scannell

A sweeping, graceful melody reflecting the elegance of the quick walking step which runs throughout the dance. A slow moving bass, excellent for the beginning player, provides a backdrop for the syncopated melody. Great for low voiced recorders, if possible. The lines should be played smoothly, diminishing the choppiness of the melody, and should be taken at a moderate tempo.

The Boatman

Playford, 1st ed. 1651

arranged by Patricia M. O'Scannell

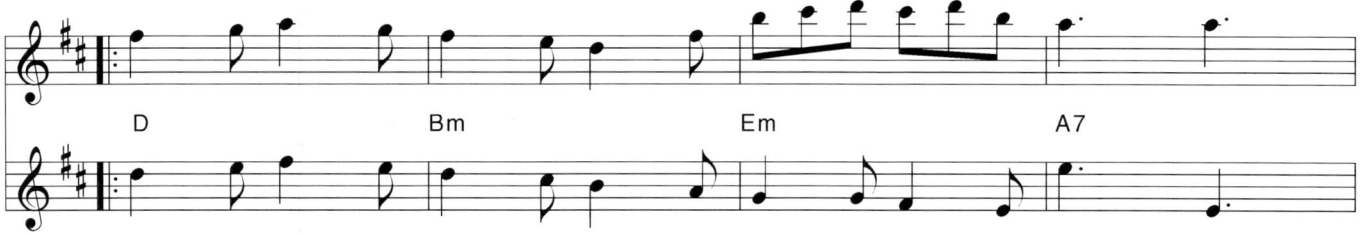

This silly, simple tune is repetitive in its sloshy 6/8 rhythms, but the image of being on the water is made humorously clear. It sounds as if the poor boatman was having quite a time being tossed about. I bring this out with a playful counter melody for alto recorder. See if you can hear him being thrown from side to side. It should be played quickly, but not too quickly, or it will lose its swing. This is a very old melody, and over the many seasons I played it at the Festival, colorful verses were created to make the tune more memorable, none of which can be repeated here.

The Bunch of Rushes

arranged by
Patricia M. O'Scannell

This haunting melody belongs to a garland dance performed many times with our local country dance ensemble. It clearly hearkens back to ancient times and perhaps to Celtic roots. I've sought to bring this out by creating a slow-moving counter melody which moves through, rather than arrives at, the cadences (this is a hallmark of Celtic harmonies, which are rooted in the concept of drones and dissonance.)

It could be played pennywhistle style, with mournful slides or smears being added on important notes. These are accomplished by sliding the involved finger or fingers over the corresponding holes, starting on the note below the note that is your destination (ie: an index finger smeared over the F♯ on a penny whistle will land on G.) Finger vibrato to add warmth on long notes in the counter melody would also be desirable. (Finger vibrato is accomplished by skipping the open hole just below your lowest fingered note, and using one or two holes below that, rhythmically opening and closing the holes with your remaining fingers. For exact fingerings, listen closely to tuning; sometimes a half-hole is enough. You want to slightly bend the pitches, and like a baroque trill, begin slowly and increase in tempo, building tension.)

Childgrove

Playford, 11th edition, 1701

arranged by Patricia M. O'Scannell

The title of this dance probably refers to a secondary and more archaic meaning of the term *childgrove*, referring to the secondary blossoms which occur after the first have faded. The image, then, is bittersweet: a last and somewhat melancholy blooming, not possessing the robustness of the blooms of early spring. Reflecting this, the melody has a modal quality which is emphasized in the counter melody. The tempo is moderately slow and steady, and lower recorders are suggested, if possible.

Christchurch Bells

Playford, 6th edition, 1679

arranged by Patricia M. O'Scannell

This is another popular dance which is both upbeat and seamless. The melody spins itself out with an accompanying descant that underlines and sometimes contrasts with it. It seems Christchurch has particularly beautiful bells. The melody by itself would sound great played on a carillon, and the leaps in the fifth, sixth and seventh measures capture the flavor of church bells ringing. Play moderately fast. with strong, but not clipped, tonguing.

The Clansman

20th c. Scottish

arranged by
Patricia M. O'Scannell

This tune definitely has its origins across the border in Scotland, where it probably began as a fiddle tune, and one can almost hear the chromatic bassline on the piano accompaniment. Set for soprano and alto recorder, it should be played at a moderate march tempo with a strong duple feeling (feeling of two).

The Comical Fellow

Thompson Collection, 1776

arranged by
Patricia M. O'Scannell

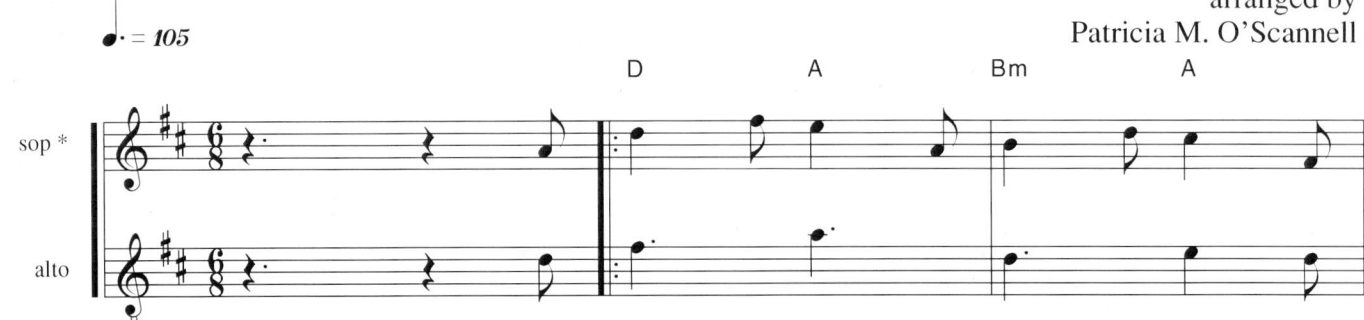
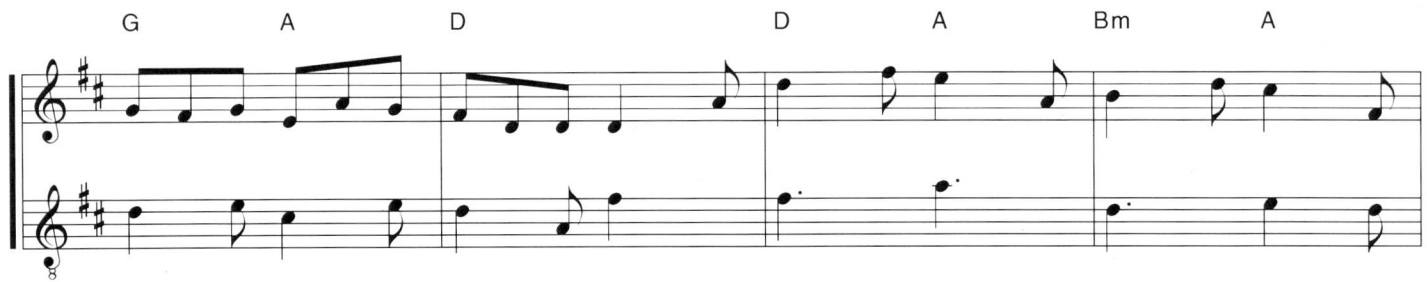
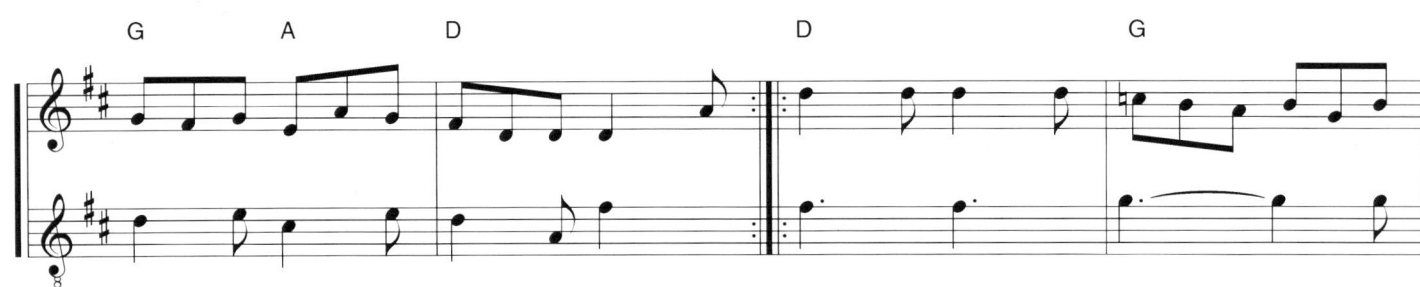

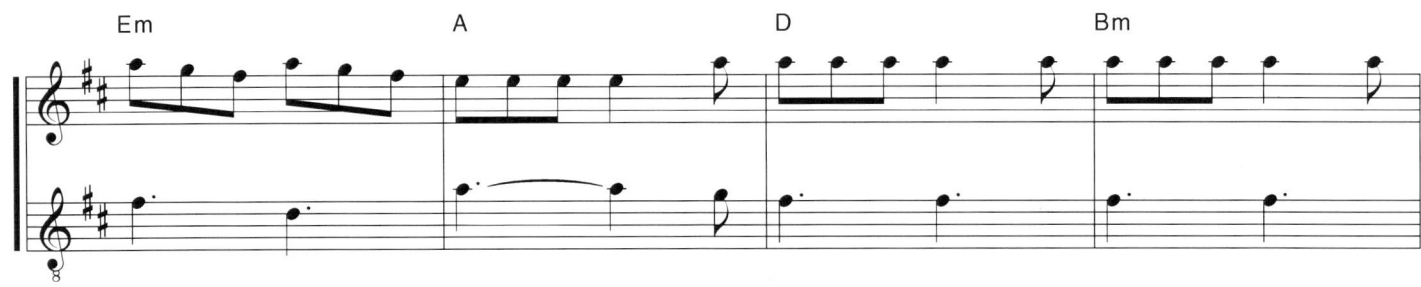

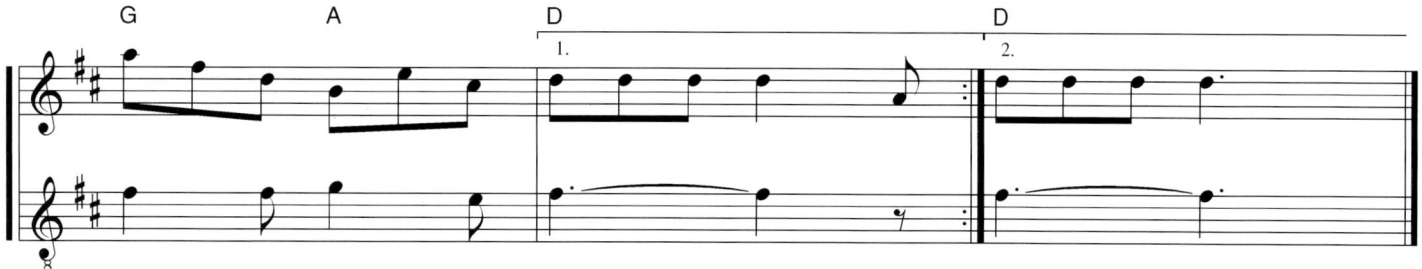

The antics of this comical fellow are evident in the topsy-turvy leaps in the melody beginning with the very first measure. The B section melody builds in tension as a sequence is repeated at increasingly higher pitches, and the tension is emphasized by a chromatically rising counter melody. It should be played at a moderate jig tempo, so that it retains its swaggering quality.

Confesse

Playford, 1st ed. 1651

arranged by
Patricia M. O'Scannell

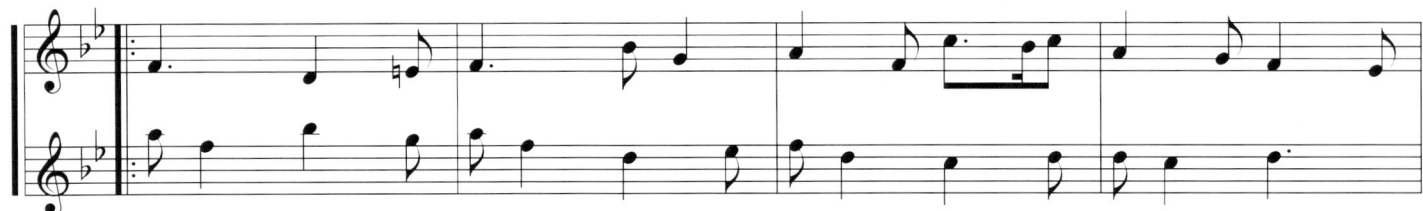

This is another very old melody finding its origins in *Playford,* and its nature is both ominous and humorous, suggesting a child's game as opposed to an actual torture session. The title could also be a dedication, referring to a person's name.

The B melody uses a snap rhythm, common in Scottish music. A snap rhythm places a short note before a long note to create a syncopation or "snap" in the melody. The dance employs a moderate walking step, and the tempo has been set accordingly.

Dick's Maggot

Playford, 11th ed. 1702

arranged by Patricia M. O'Scannell

In this wistfully happy tune, the title refers to an archaic use of the word, meaning a whimsy, odd notion, or surprise. The counterpoint engages with the melody, echoing back many of its lively motives, and the slow-moving bass line provides a backdrop and continuity for the other rapidly weaving lines. A light, quick walking-step is employed, but the melody should remain smooth and gentle.

Epping Forest

Playford, 4th edition, 1670

arranged by Patricia M. O'Scannell

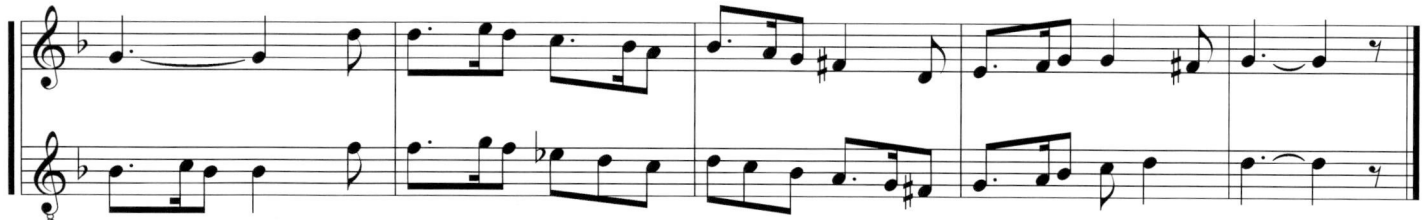

This frolicsome tune originates in the Renaissance, when triple meter ruled the land. The dance employs the familiar circle figure, which is one of the most ancient figures to appear in the country dance form. The melody has a chameleon-like character and can be played from a slow-walking to a quick-walking tempo. Articulations should be light and crisp.

Easter Thursday

The Complete English Dancing Master, 1733

arranged by
Patricia M. O'Scannell

This melody is hopeful and forward reaching, a suitable companion to the holiday from which it takes its name. This is one of the new dances Carl was working on for his book, and I was profoundly moved by the sincerity of the tune. It should be played at a relaxed walking tempo, not too fast, and the recorders should use gentle articulations and lots of air for these sweeping melodies.

Fain I Would

Playford, 1st edition, 1651

arranged by
Patricia M. O'Scannell

This has been a favorite among many early dance ensembles I have accompanied over the years. It has a melancholic melody which is preferably played at a slower tempo, so that the cascading sixteenth note pattern retains its graceful quality and does not appear rushed. It should be played with gentle tonguing and lots of air, so that its beautiful and lyrical melody can soar.

The Fair Quaker of Deal

arranged by
Patricia M. O'Scannell

These fair folk were apparently an affable bunch: the melody is somewhat innocuous but pleasant, as it rambles along. It should not be taken at more than a medium skipping tempo. Set for two soprano recorders, it could as well be played on two pennywhistles, as the key of D is perfect for the standard D pennywhistle. The clear, bright timbre of the high recorders will help give this melody the energy it needs to be carried off well.

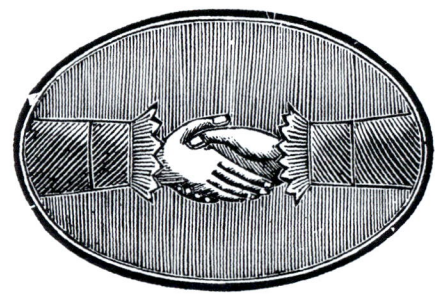

The Female Saylor

Essex, 1710

arranged by
Patricia M. O'Scannell

Outside of the wonderful imagery in the title, depicting women of Eighteenth century England engaging in non-traditional nautical activities, this tune also bears the melody of the beautiful English carol, *Masters in This Hall*. It is ironic to find a carol melody for an instrumental tune, as the term carol originally denoted dances that were sung. This is a cheerful and robust melody and should be played at a tempo corresponding to the familiar carol. It will sound nice on either high or low recorders.

Fentalarich

20th c. tune by Fred Grimshaw
20th c. dance by Joyce Walker

arranged by Patricia M. O'Scannell

"Nancy's Fancy"

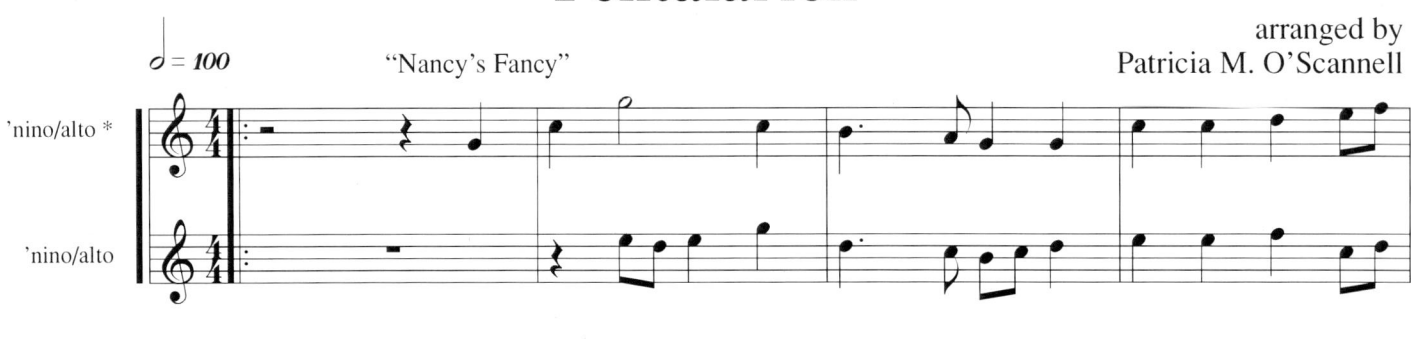
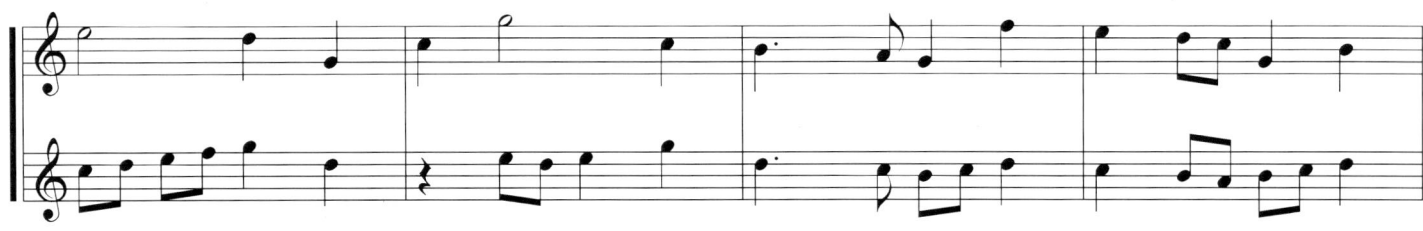

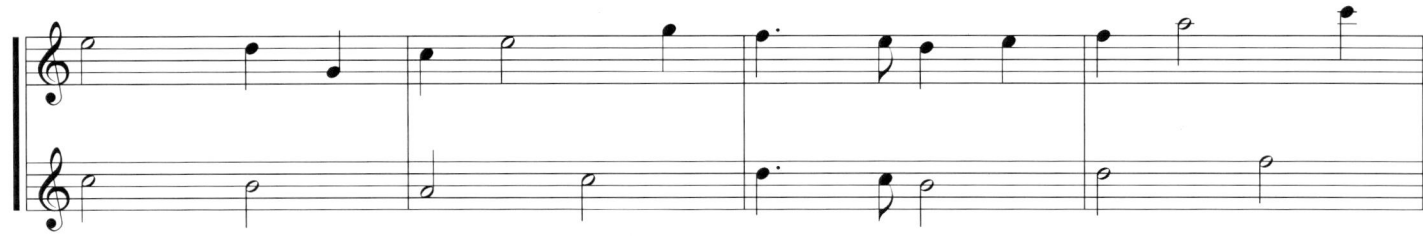

This melody is gracious and inviting. It can be played from a moderate to a quicker tempo, but the dance moves along in a swift walking gait. Either way, the melody is typical of this genre and brings to mind the gentle sound of long skirts as they swept the dance floor. The counter-melody gives rhythmic interest to the squareness of the duple meter. The tune should sound relaxed and friendly and be executed playfully.

Gathering Peascods

Playford, 1st edition, 1651

arranged by
Patricia M. O'Scannell

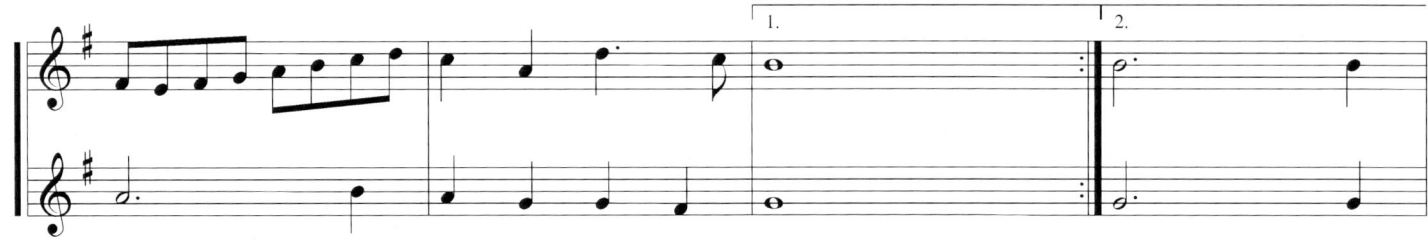

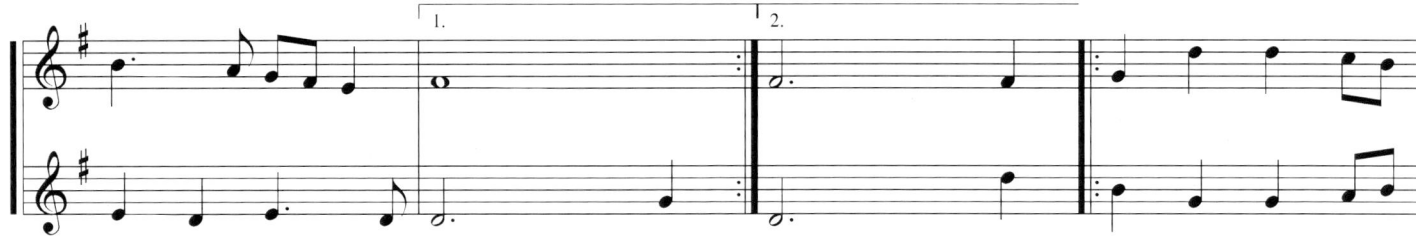

This is surely one of the first dances to be taught to the aspiring country dancer, and as such, is familiar to even the most casual dabbler. It is a circle dance, and when performed, has the look of a Breughel painting come to life. The tune is lively and lighthearted, and sounds best when it is musically "tossed off". Have fun with it. Not too fast though; dancers have to move quickly in a circle holding hands! I think high recorders are more suitable than low for the flavor of the melody.

Hambleton's Round O

Young, 2nd edition, vol. II, 1714

arranged by
Patricia M. O'Scannell

This is a brisk and jovial melody and has a sound reminiscent of chamber music with courtly origins. A strong instrument on the bass-line would be excellent (violin would work, due to the range of the recorders), but the bass-line is also a great opportunity for a beginning player to get in on some ensemble playing. Take it at a medium-fast tempo and use trills at cadences if you like. (Remember: Baroque trills begin on the note above.)

The Hen and All Her Broth

20th c.

arranged by
Patricia M. O'Scannell

This melody hints at an Irish origin, and it is like many jigs from that country. Perhaps it came into the genre via Scotland, but, by providing a rambling descant line, I have given it a very non-Celtic treatment. (In traditional Irish and Scottish music, instruments generally double on the melody unless providing drones or chords.) The descant is an endless cascade of eighth notes, and it is a foil to the galumpfing melody. Set for two soprano recorders, it would also work well on two pennywhistles. Take it at a medium to slow jig tempo.

The Hole in the Wall

Playford, 2nd edition, pt.II, 1698

arranged by
Patricia M. O'Scannell

This has to be one of the true gems of English country dance melodies. With an elegance suggestive of a large formal ballroom and an orchestra playing in the more courtly or classical style (as opposed to the earthier style of the countryside), this melody is to traditional folk melodies what O'Carolan's tunes were to traditional Irish dance tunes. Baroque embellishments (such as trills) are completely appropriate here (start on the note above; trills should increase in speed to the cadence). If a harpsichord were available, I would definitely use it on this tune. A slow walking tempo is advisable. Play one or the other of the top two lines for variety, but not both together.

In the Fields of Frost and Snow

Young, 1st edition, vol. II, c.1713
arranged by Patricia M. O'Scannell

The bleakness of winter is clearly felt in this melody. It is whimsical and contemplative, and one can somehow sense the silence of the surrounding snow-covered fields. Play it slowly with lots of breath support and use gentle, even tonguing.

Jack's Health

Playford, 6th edition, 1679

arranged by Patricia M. O'Scannell

This earthy tune definitely captures the flavor of a health or toast, with its impromptu feel. A comical descant line is poised above the ribald melody. The bass line, with its chromatically-descending melody, has the flavor of the piano accompaniments that dominated the sound of 19th century dance accompaniment. It would work equally well on high or low consort. Take it at a medium to fast tempo.

Jack's Maggot

Playford, 11th edition, 1702

arranged by
Patricia M. O'Scannell

The term maggot refers to a type of dance, so there is little mystery here as to the meaning of the title. The melody is in a quick march-like duple, and resembles the tune *Newcastle* in many ways. I have written another part in a similar range, and have used some simple counterpoint to weave the second melody around the first. It is set for two soprano recorders but would work very nicely on two D pennywhistles.

Joy After Sorrow

Young, 4th edition, vol. II, 1728

arranged by
Patricia M. O'Scannell

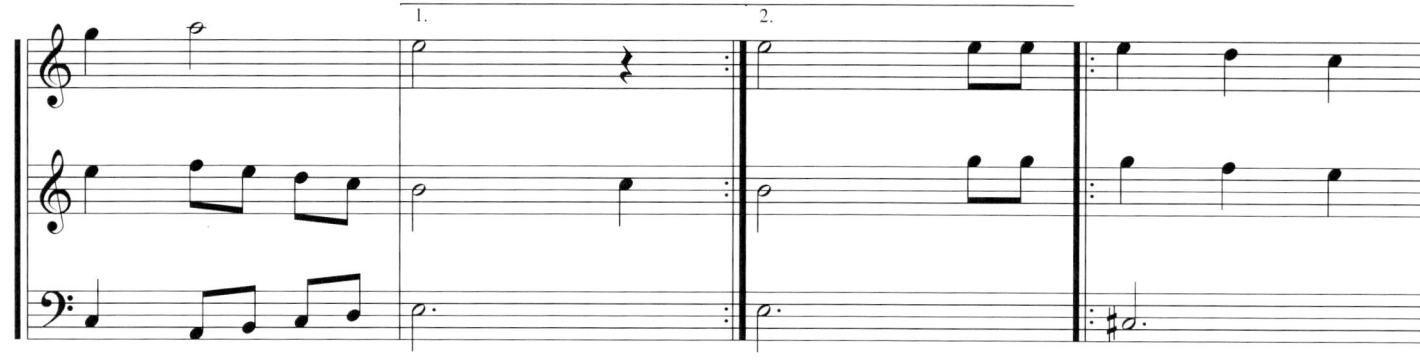
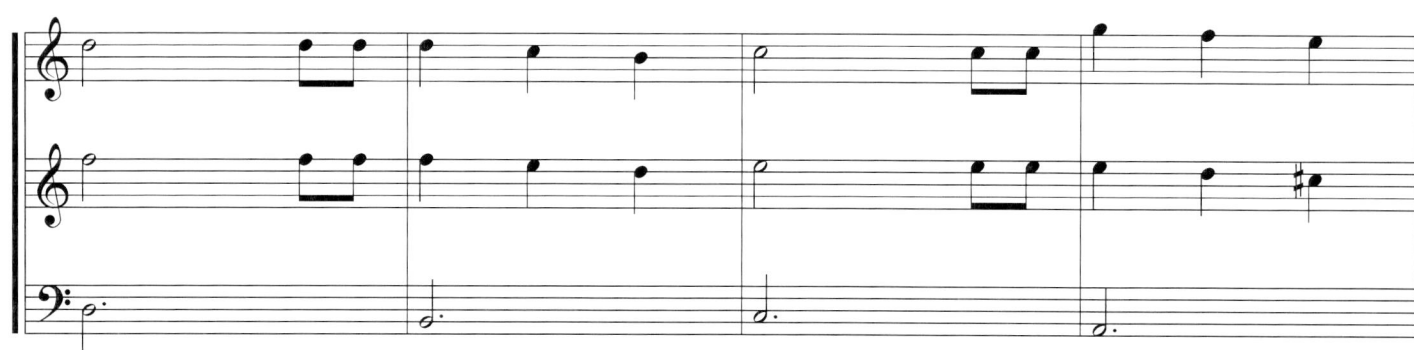

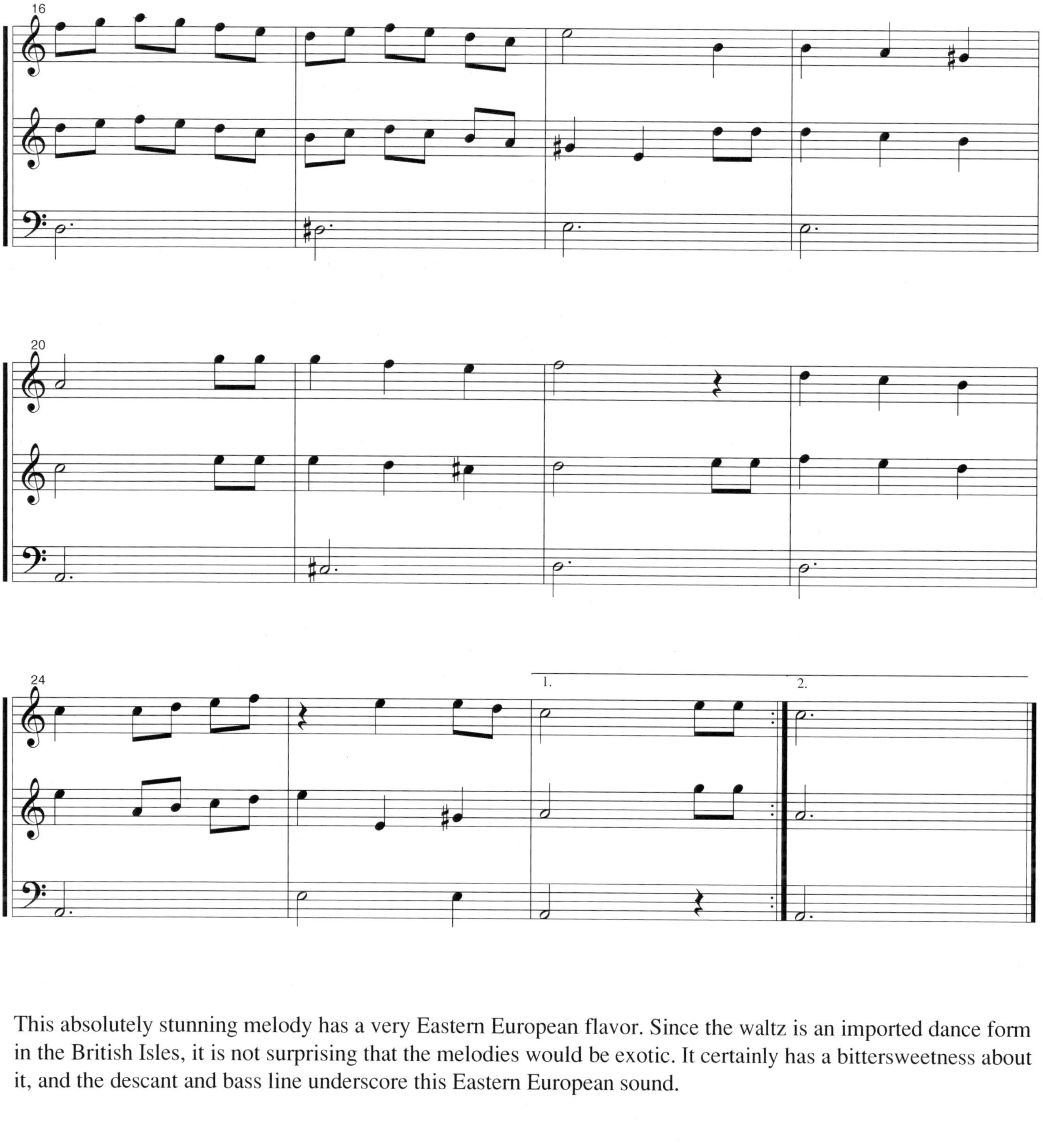

This absolutely stunning melody has a very Eastern European flavor. Since the waltz is an imported dance form in the British Isles, it is not surprising that the melodies would be exotic. It certainly has a bittersweetness about it, and the descant and bass line underscore this Eastern European sound.

Knole Park

Bishop, 1788

arranged by
Patricia M. O'Scannell

This is another cream-of-the-crop country dance melody, with all the charm and formality befitting a grand ball. The lyrical B section truly soars, and the descant should be played with the same delicacy and finesse. The tune has an introductory feeling, as if it were meant to be played as the first dance of the evening. Play it smoothly, evenly, and at a moderate tempo.

Lord Howe's Jig

Thompson Collection, 1777

arranged by Patricia M. O'Scannell

This romping jig is lots of fun to play on either recorders or pennywhistles. The descant line forms a duet at the interval of a sixth which follows the rhythm of the melody. Relax and use gentle tonguing or, better yet, play pennywhistle style with no tonguing. Practicing pieces without using the tongue is an excellent exercise to clean up sloppy fingerings. Add the articulation back in when the notes can be played perfectly and evenly. Moderate jig tempo.

Long Live London

Pat Shaw, 1971

arranged by Patricia M. O'Scannell

This contemporary melody, written by Pat Shaw, has a bold and decisive flavor. I have added divisions to embellish the original melody. Its inherent humor is emphasized by a rambling chromatic bass line, with a playfully teasing descant. Play the bass line legato (smoothly, with even tonguing) and at a brisk tempo.

Love's Triumph

Young, 1st edition, vol. II, 1713

arranged by
Patricia M. O'Scannell

40

This is a gentle tune that speaks of the tenderness of love's beginnings. It must be played at a moderately slow tempo, or the quarter note/half note motive will lose its elegance. It has quite a wide range, so this melody line is for the experienced player. The large leaps in the B melody must be carefully placed. (Relax the face and use differing vowel colors: ah and oh in the low range, ee and ay in the high range. Experiment! What facial shape makes the notes come out most clearly?) Use gentle articulations.

Lulle Me Beyond Thee

Playford, 1st edition, 1651

arranged by Patricia M. O'Scannell

I will always treasure this as one of the dances performed my first year at the Oregon Shakespeare Festival, when Carl was temporary choreographer. The title is mysterious and intriguing, and the melody does have the quality of a lullabye, as the title suggests. There is also a magical quality, when the melody is taken more slowly. A slow, walking tempo is best and allows the music to express itself fully.

Mr. Beveridge's Maggot

Playford, 9th edition, 1695

arranged by Patricia M. O'Scannell

Yes, maggots abound in this recorder edition! Here is another 6/8 dance, this one so decidedly in three. The melody is sophisticated and courtly and would benefit from a continuo section. [*Continuo*: the part of a baroque ensemble playing the bass line and chords.] A lower countermelody and bass line have been added to create a trio. Trills and other Baroque ornamentation would be appropriate here. The distance between the soprano and bass recorders creates a deeper, more orchestral sound.

Mr. Cosgill's Delight

Young, vol. III, 1728

arranged by
Patricia M. O'Scannell

This delightful melody is both lighthearted and intricate. I've added an alternate melody line, one with lots more notes for fun on repeats. Don't play the two melody lines together, or you will be in for a big surprise. As you become more familiar with the melody, use the opportunity to try and make up your own divisions.
[*Divisions*: a Renaissance term meaning to elaborate on the melody by dividing long notes into shorter values.]
The bass line is very simple: perfect for the beginner.

Mr. Isaac's Maggot

Playford, 9th edition, 1651

arranged by
Patricia M. O'Scannell

Another delicate melody suitable for the formal ballroom and lending itself to a moderate tempo. The tonguing should be light and precise, with big breaths to carry through the long, elegant phrases. A counter-melody for alto recorder spins itself around the soprano part and creates a pleasing duet.

Mrs. Savage's Whim

Young, 1st edition, vol. II, 1713

arranged by Patricia M. O'Scannell

Who was this Mrs. Savage? She must have been truly special or the composer wouldn't have wasted such a clever melody on her. The tune has a modal or minor feeling, and it would be very romantic played on hammer dulcimer. The pure clarity of the recorder is perfect for this tune, which is brisk and haughty. Play with strong articulations and have fun with the syncopated bass line. (The top two lines are in three, and the bottom is in two!)

Orleans Baffled

Young, 2nd edition, vol. II, 1714

arranged by
Patricia M. O'Scannell

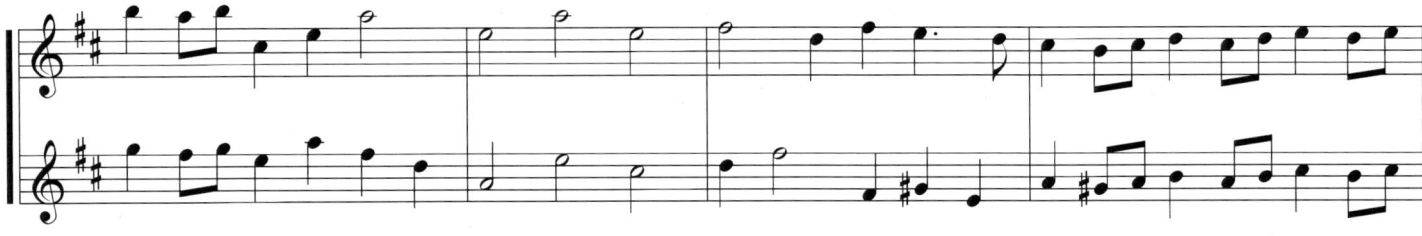

This tune is another favorite among dancers and has some of the flavor of *The Bishop*. It is bold and daring, needing to be played with lots of energy. The tune is zippy and should be played with strong articulations to avoid sounding muddy. The duet is for high or low recorders, either working well, and each adding a different interpretation to this setting.

Parson's Farewell

Playford, 1st edition, 1651

arranged by
Patricia M. O'Scannell

This melody retains a sad wistfulness that befits the occasion of friends departing. Perhaps the tune and dance were composed as a good-bye present to the well-loved Parson. This little duet for soprano and alto recorders should be played at a moderate tempo, with light tonguing. (I find that an L, or flipped R tonguing are best.)

St. Andrew's Fair

arranged by
Patricia M. O'Scannell

♩. = 100

alto

alto/ten *

This is a bouncy, sprightly little tune with melodic material that conjures up a scene of bustling activity and sounds almost like a fanfare in many places. It is in a medium duple meter, and should be played with plenty of strong articulation. Make sure that the first note in every group of three eighth notes has a stronger tonguing than the other two, and this will keep the eighth-note passages from sounding too notey.

St. Margaret's Hill

Young, 2nd edition, vol. II, 1714

arranged by
Patricia M. O'Scannell

The location in the title must be a place of great beauty, for the melody is sweet and faerie-like. You can almost see the gathering mist, as the dancers join hands. Play with lots of feeling and give these magnificently long phrases plenty of air. Articulation should be light. It can be played on low or high recorders, although the low ensemble may bring out the mysterious quality of the melody more effectively.

Sellinger's Round I.

Playford, 4th edition, 1670

arranged by
Patricia M. O'Scannell

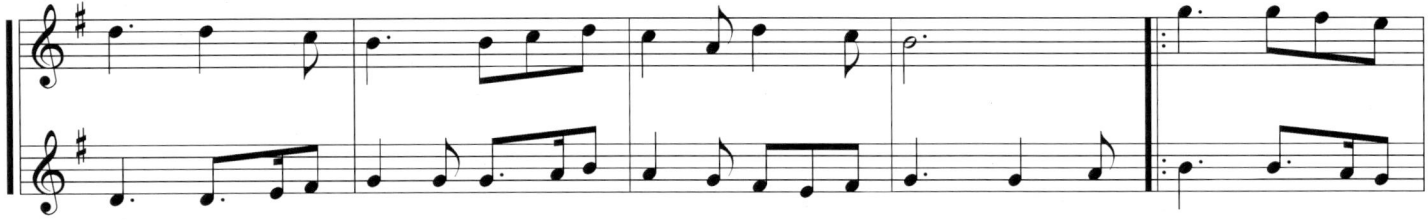
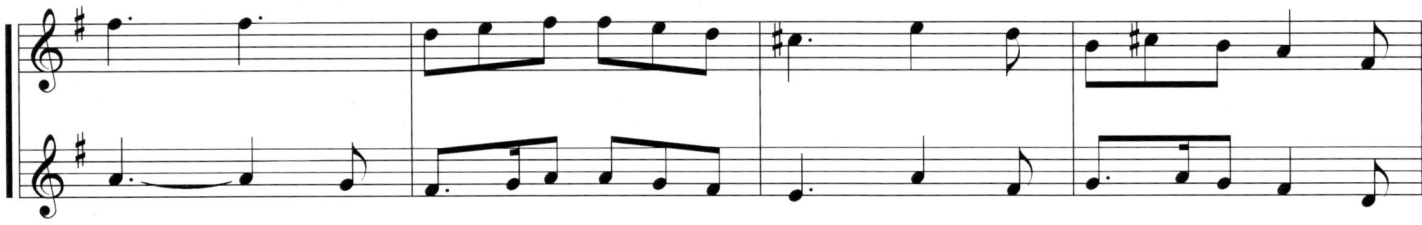

Here is another favorite in the country dance community. This one also has very simple figures, and is often taught to beginners. It is a typical Renaissance country dance melody, and lends itself to a medium fast tempo. In the first version, I have put the melody below the descant, whereas in the second version the melody appears above, with another soprano in a closer harmony below. The tune has a processional feeling, with a stateliness that balances the simplicity of the dance well.

Sellinger's Round II.

Playford, 4th edition, 1670

arranged by Patricia M. O'Scannell

In this alternate setting, the melody appears in the top line.

Spring Garden

Playford, 3rd edition, 1665

arranged by Patricia M. O'Scannell

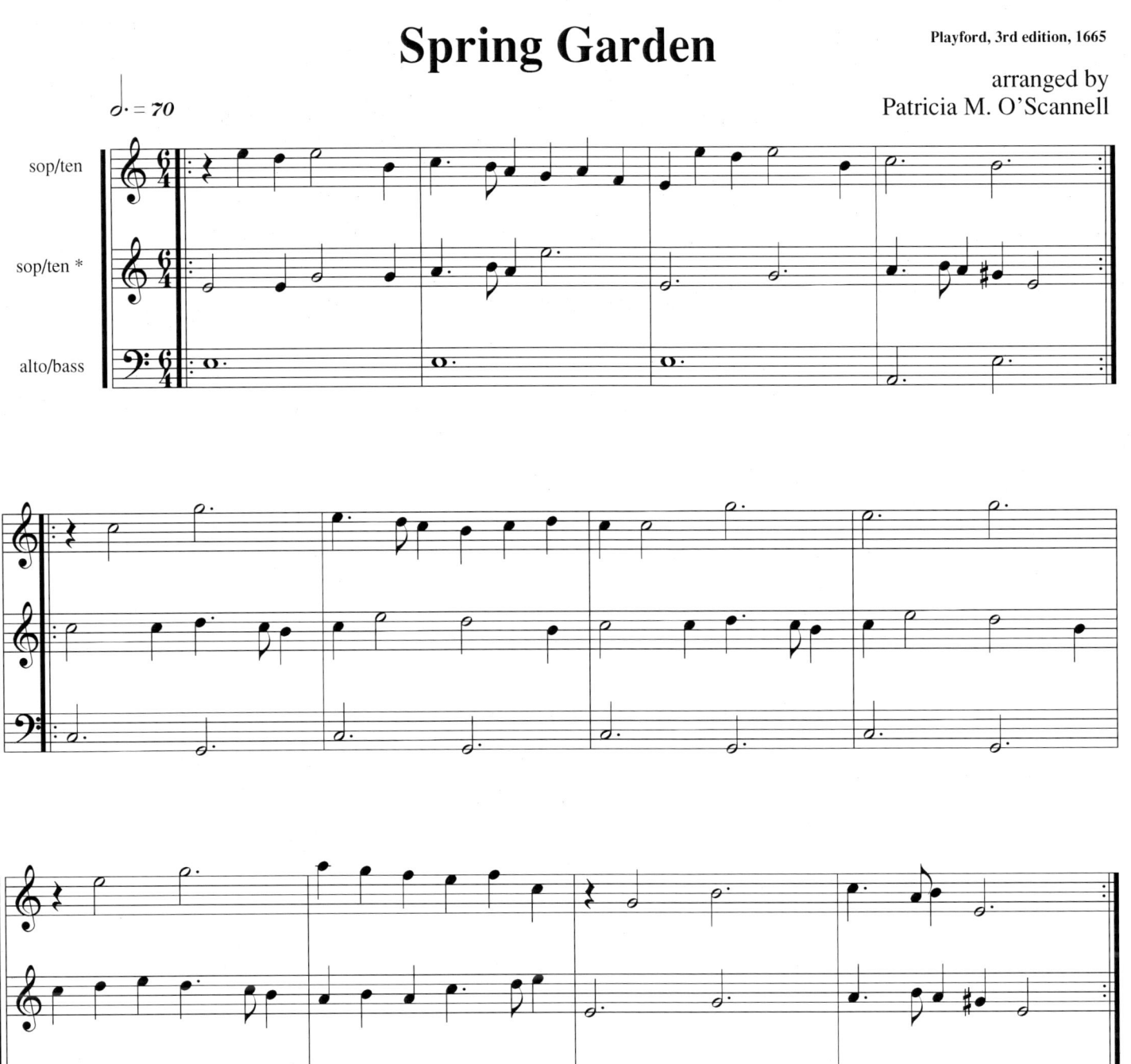

In a place that is often overcast and cloudy, the coming of spring is a very important event. In addition, seasonal changes have, for thousands of years, been the centerpiece for British pre-Christian ritual. Rather than going for the obvious, this melody holds within it all of the promise of spring. I have written a descant and very simple bass line. Use deep breaths to sustain these long notes, and play slowly and smoothly throughout.

Tribute to the Borders

Scottish, possibly 20th century

arranged by Patricia M. O'Scannell

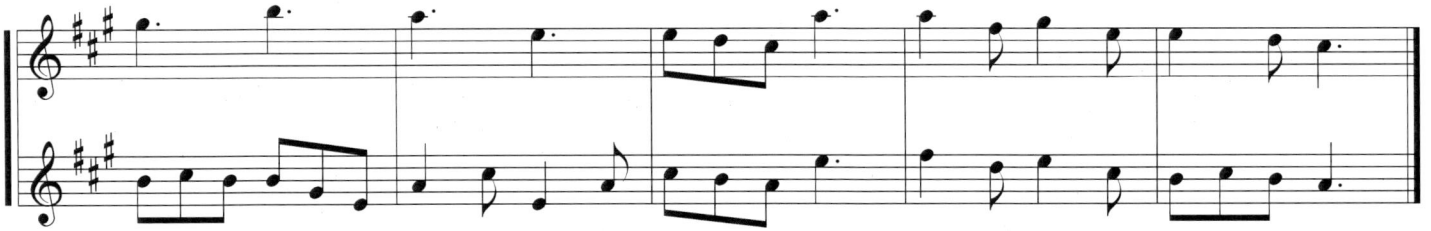

The origins of this tune are easily felt and well expressed in the title, which refers to a region along the Scottish-English border, known as Northumbria. It sounds as if the tribute were being performed on horseback, with all its galloping rhythms. Use strong articulations, and play at a moderately fast (galloping) tempo. Two pennywhistles in D would also work quite well.

Sun Assembly

Thompson Collection, 1757
arranged by
Patricia M. O'Scannell

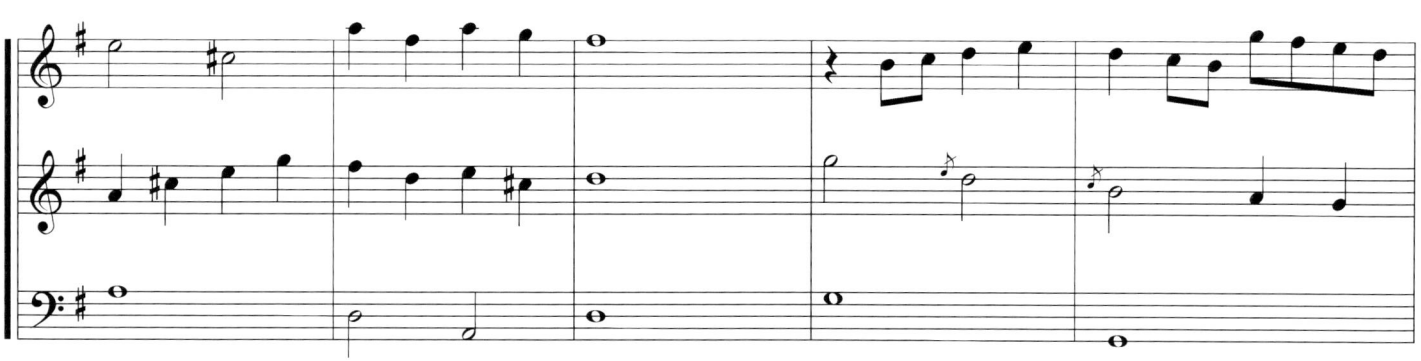

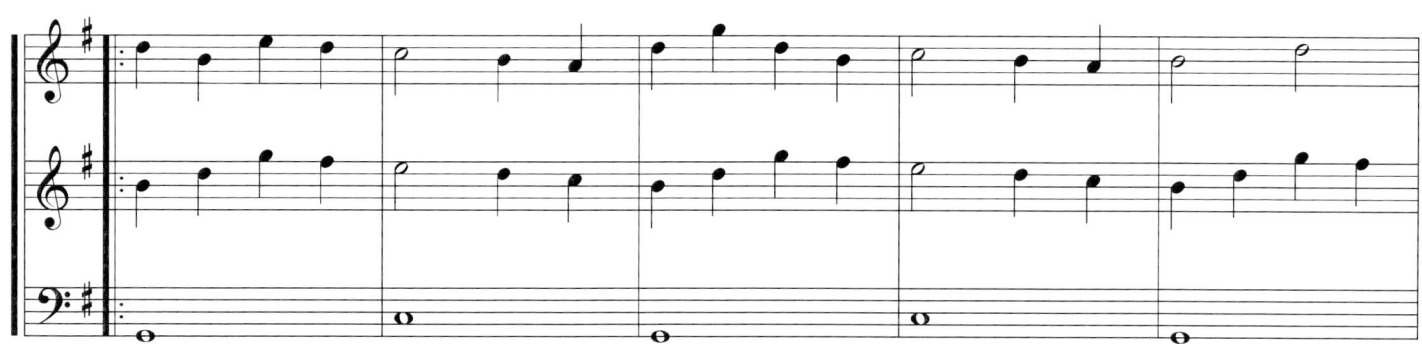

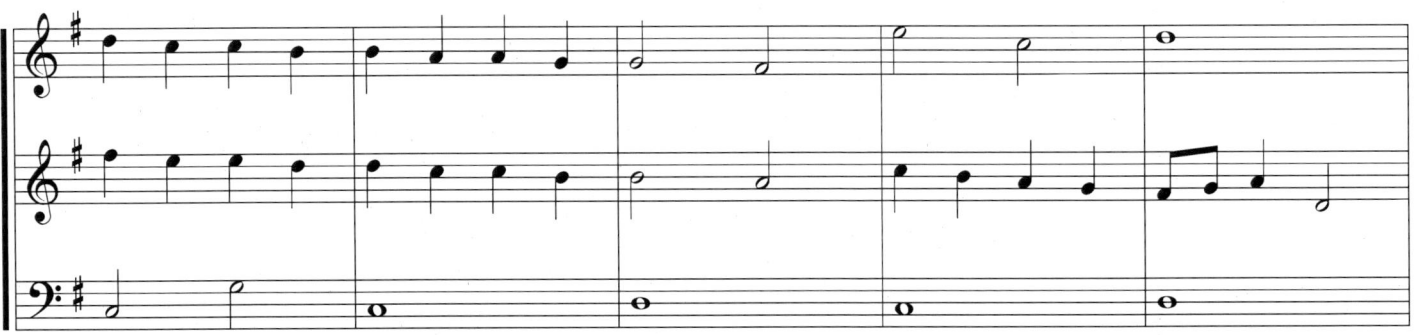

I always think of Carl when I hear this uplifting melody. I can see his light blond hair and bright blue eyes and feel the generosity of spirit which characterized his interpretation of this English country dance. Carl was very particular that the single-note grace notes be executed exactly as written, no faster (as eighth-note appogiaturas). Play the melody line emphatically and with conviction.

The Spring

Bray, 1699
arranged by
Patricia M. O'Scannell

Here is another melody of great breadth and beauty, employing a moderate walking tempo, with a floating descant poised above the melody. Use gentle tonguings. The drone-like tenor line should be played in combination, with the top two parts first, to build tension. On the second or third time around, have the bass enter. The drone can drop out or stay in, depending on the desired effect.

Trip to Paris I.

Young, vol. III, 1728

arranged by
Patricia M. O'Scannell

This tune has a clearly continental sound, as if someone imported it, with the very different flavor of a French country dance melody. Many such tunes came to Britain in the Renaissance via numerous courtly dance arrangements that drew upon music of the French countryside, albeit smoothed over into beautiful polyphonic settings (*polyphonic*: more than one line). An actual trip to Paris would not have been necessary to hear such continental influences. It is in a sprightly duple meter, but keep the articulation smooth and light and the phrases long. I have composed a more ornate version of the melody which can alternate with the counter melody, to create an ever changing duet.

Trip to Paris II.

Young, vol. III, 1728

arranged by Patricia M. O'Scannell

In this arrangement I've placed the melody above, with the familiar frolicking countermelody for the alto recorder. To this has been added a very simple but suprisingly satisfying bass line, great for the beginner. The same rules used in Trip to Paris I apply to articulation and tempo, but the bass line is an excellent opportunity to work on tone, the most important component of recorder technique.

www.melbay.com